BALLET

LISA DILLMAN

Heinemann Library
Chicago, Illinois

© 2006 Heinemann Library
a division of Reed Elsevier Inc.
Chicago, Illinois

Customer Service   888–454–2279

Visit our website at www.heinemannlibrary.com

Photo research by Jill Birschbach
Designed by Joanna Turner
Originated by Ambassador Litho Ltd.
Printed in China by WKT Company Ltd.

10 09 08 07 06
10 9 8 7 6 5 4 3 2 1

Library of Congress Cataloging-in-Publication Data

Dillman, Lisa, 1957-
 Ballet / by Lisa Dillman.
    v. cm. — (Get going! hobbies)
 Contents: What is ballet? — Ballet : yesterday and today — Getting started — Perfecting your placement — The five basic ballet positions — Using the barre — Center practice — The Stage and Dancing on Pointe — Home practice — Feeling the music — Playing a role — Recitals and performances — An international art form.
 ISBN 1-4034-6115-5 (Hardcover) — ISBN 1-4034-6122-8 (Paperback)
 1. Ballet—Juvenile literature. [1. Ballet.] I. Title. II. Series.
 GV1787.5.D55 2004
 792.8—dc22

                            2003025498

Acknowledgments
The author and publisher are grateful to the following for permission to reproduce copyright material: p. 4 Paul A. Sauders/Corbis; pp. 5, 9, 10, 11, 12, 13, 14, 15, 16a-c, 19a-b, 20, 21, 23, 24, 25t, 27b Robert Lifson/Heinemann Library; p. 6 Giraudon/ Art Resource, NY; p. 7t Bettmann/Corbis; p. 7b, 19c Reuters/Corbis; p. 8 Stone/Getty Images; p. 16d Christopher Cormack/Corbis; p. 17 Tom Pantages; p. 22 Robbie Jack/Corbis; p. 25b Morton Beebe/Corbis; p. 27t Steve Raymer/Corbis; p. 28t Cardinale Stephane/Corbis Sygma; p. 28b Dean Conger/Corbis; p. 29a Julie Lemberger/Corbis; p. 29b Ann Johansson/Corbis; p. 29c Bob Krist/Corbis

Cover photograph of ballet dancers by Misha Japaridze/AP Wide World Photos

Special thanks to Courtney Combs Docter for her expert comments that were used to complete this book.

CONTENTS

Some words are shown in bold, **like this.** You can find out what they mean by looking in the glossary.

Ballet is a dance form that originated in Italy and became popular in the French court of King Louis XIV about 300 years ago. The word *ballet* is French but comes from the Italian word *ballare,* which means "to dance." Ballet consists of graceful movements, quick spins, high jumps, and leaps. Sometimes, the dancers seem to float through the air! Ballet is a very **athletic** and gymnastic art form, but dancers are trained to make it seem effortless.

This ballerina is about to perform a dance known as a variation.

Female ballet dancers, who are also called ballerinas, dance on the tips of their toes in special footwear called **pointe shoes** or toe shoes. Children cannot begin to dance in these shoes until their **technique** is strong and the bones of their feet are fully formed.

FAMOUS BALLETS

The following are some of the best-known classical ballets:

Coppélia is the story of a doll that comes to life.
Don Quixote describes the adventures of a well-intentioned fool who loves life and lives in a dream world.
Giselle is the sad tale of passionate love and early death.
Sleeping Beauty tells of a girl who falls asleep for 100 years before being awakened by a prince.
Swan Lake is a fantasy of love and magic.
The Firebird is about a magical bird that must grant a favor to anyone who is able to take one of its feathers.
The Nutcracker is a holiday favorite based on a German story.

LEARNING AND PRACTICING AT THE STUDIO

This book explains how to begin learning ballet, but you cannot learn how to dance from a book. Beginner dancers study with dance teachers in private lessons and group classes. Becoming a **professional** dancer takes years of hard work and daily practice.

Ballet classes are held in large practice rooms called studios. A typical ballet studio has wooden floors, a ballet **barre,** and mirrored walls. The mirrors help students to see and correct their movements. The classes can be fun because they give you the chance to watch and perform for other student dancers.

Learning ballet means that you will be using your body in new ways. As a result, it is important that you study with a qualified teacher who will monitor your progress, help you avoid injuries, and make sure you perform the movements correctly.

It is important that you learn ballet from a trained teacher who can show you the proper way to dance.

"The trained dancer must not only have grace and elegance, but also the leap of an Olympic hurdler, the balance of a tightrope walker, and panther-like strength and agility."—Camilla Jessel, author of *Ballet School*

REVERENCE

At the end of a ballet class, dancers perform a reverence, which is a bow of thanks to their teacher and musical **accompanist.**

BALLET: YESTERDAY AND TODAY

Although ballet began in Italy in the 1400s, it is an art form that is always changing. Throughout European history, as society and social styles changed, so did ballet.

THE BEGINNINGS OF BALLET

The earliest form of ballet was performed for **royalty.** It combined music, singing, painting, dancing, and poetry. The dancers wore large, heavy costumes and performed in front of beautifully painted stage scenery.

This painting shows a performance in France in 1674.

An early form of ballet was performed in Paris, France, in 1581. It was created for a wedding celebration and performed for an audience of 10,000 people. France's King Louis XIV established the first school of ballet in 1661. The five basic ballet positions were defined there. In those days ordinary people and women were not allowed to perform. Men of royalty played all the roles. This changed over time and others began to train for the ballet. The first ballet performance by a woman was in 1681.

THE BEGINNINGS OF MODERN BALLET

Many people were instrumental in developing ballet from its early stages. Jean-Georges Noverre (1727–1810) created a ballet style called *ballet d'action.* It was natural, emotionally expressive, and meant to tell a story. Carlo Blasis (1797–1878), an Italian, was perhaps the most important ballet teacher of the 1800s. In his books he outlined methods of teaching and performing ballet. These ideas would become the basis of modern ballet styles.

Auguste Bournonville (1805–1879), a **choreographer** at the Royal Danish Ballet, traveled the world and created ballets for people in Scotland, Belgium, Italy, and the Middle East. In the late 1800s, a Frenchman named Marius Petipa (1819–1910) was the **ballet master** of the Imperial Russian Ballet. He perfected a form of story ballet that combined **traditional** ballet movements with **mimed** scenes.

In 1934 George Balanchine and Lincoln Kirstein founded the School of American Ballet in New York City. In the 1940s two great ballet companies opened in New York, the American Ballet Theater and the New York City Ballet. Since the mid-1900s many successful ballet **companies** have sprung up in cities across the United States and around the world.

George Balanchine is shown here with a partner in 1935.

CONTEMPORARY BALLET

As they have for hundreds of years, audiences today enjoy the beauty of ballet. Like other art forms, today's ballet can focus on a theme or mood. Sometimes ballet does not tell a story. Instead it is an **interpretation** of music.

Because of the influence of younger audiences, **contemporary** ballet is often performed not to classical music but to rock and roll or jazz. There is also more emphasis on **athleticism** and new ballet forms. Today's dance **professionals** use both the traditional ballet positions and the new movements that reflect our modern world.

These dancers attended a tryout for a chance to study at the American School of Ballet.

Learning ballet is fun, but it can also be hard work. In the beginning of your ballet training, you will probably take only one class per week. As you learn more and improve your skills, you may want to take your study further. Teenagers who wish to become **professional** ballet dancers take classes and practice every day.

BALLET GROOMING TIPS

Whether you are a student taking your first ballet class or a professional who has been dancing for years, good grooming and proper dress are important parts of dance preparation.

- Keep your fingernails short and clean.

- Girls should use hair spray and/or hair nets to keep hair up and back. If you have short hair, pin it back or wear a headband. If you have long hair, pin it up in a bun or a twist.

- Boys may use a tennis headband if needed to keep hair out of the face.

- Remove any jewelry before you begin your ballet practice.

- If you wear glasses, you should secure them with a stretch-band. These are available at sporting goods stores.

Leotard

Tights

Ballet slippers

These are typical ballet practice clothes.

DRESSING FOR DANCE

You will need the right shoes and clothing to take ballet classes. Both boys and girls wear tights to practice and perform ballet. These are made of a stretchy material that fits snugly to the body and allows easy movement. Girls wear a **leotard**, while boys wear a clean white T-shirt.

SHOES

Dancers must always feel secure in their shoes. Their shoes must fit well and stay on. Your dance teacher can help you decide which type of shoe is best for you.

Ballet slippers are soft leather or canvas shoes that fit snugly and move easily with the foot. They are secured by ribbons or elastic and usually have soft soles. *Pointe shoes* are used by advanced female dancers who are able to dance on the tips of their toes. This type of shoe is made from a combination of satin, canvas, leather, and glue. The style of the shoe and the hardness of the sole are specially designed for the individual dancer's feet. These shoes are secured by ribbons that cross over the ankle and tie neatly on the inside of the ankle.

Character shoes have hard soles and look like street shoes. They are used in folk or ethnic dances. *Jazz shoes* can have hard or soft soles and can look like shoes, boots, or sneakers. They are constructed so that the shoe remains **flexible** and the dancer can point his or her toes easily.

character shoes

tap shoes

ballet slippers

pointe shoes

jazz shoes

The kind of shoe you will need depends on the type of dancing you plan to study.

Ballet is all about strength and grace. To perform ballet movements and positions, you also need proper body **alignment.** To do this you must strengthen all your muscles, including the ones that help you stand up straight. Your teacher will show you ways to improve your **placement.**

TIPS TO IMPROVE YOUR ALIGNMENT

Good alignment is something you can work on every day whether you practice ballet or not. If you keep the following rules in mind and practice them when you are walking, you will have a head start on the proper alignment you need for ballet.

1 Make sure your weight is evenly on both feet. You should feel the weight equally on both feet.

2 Align the front of your hipbones over the front of your heels, making an imaginary rectangle so that your weight is placed straight down. Be careful not to push your knees back into a **hyperextended** position.

3 Place your shoulders over the fronts of your hipbones, making a second imaginary rectangle that will align the spine.

4 Your head should rise gently upward and forward so that the back of your neck lengthens and your weight is lifted off your hips. Do not lift your chin or tuck it toward your neck.

5 Feel the ribs open and the shoulders relax so that rib cage expands and releases in every direction with each breath.

6 Remember to breathe!

Notice the straight line of this dancer's body.

IMPROVING YOUR TURNOUT

Ballet creates a sense of freedom or the feeling of flight by using open movements. To develop their range of motion and create graceful body movements, ballet dancers turn their legs out from the hip. This is known as **turnout.** Turnout is one of the things that separates ballet from other dance forms.

Many ballet teachers find this exercise useful.

1 Lie on the floor with your spine straight, long, and relaxed. Your arms should be relaxed at your side.

2 Bring your feet to a parallel position so that your heels and the toes on each foot touch.

3 Flex your toes up toward the ceiling, keeping them in contact with one another.

4 Turn your feet so your little toes rotate toward the floor.

5 Rotate your legs back to the parallel position with toes pointed.

ANOTHER TURNOUT EXERCISE

When you have done the exercise several times, reverse the process, as described below.

1 Turn your toes out in the pointed position.

2 Flex your feet with your toes turned out.

3 Rotate to a parallel position while your feet are still flexed.

4 Point your feet while keeping them in the parallel position.

5 Repeat several times.

With proper turnout, the legs turn out from the hips. The exercises on this page will help you improve turnout.

Ballet is made up of five basic positions that can be combined in various ways to create many different movements. Every ballet step begins and ends with one of these positions.

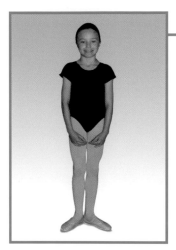

First Position. In first position, your heels are touching and your toes are turned out to the side. Your arms are extended forward. Your hands should be slightly apart and your elbows should be open.

Second Position. Your feet should be shoulder-width apart and turned out to the sides. Make sure your weight is placed evenly on both feet. Your arms should be open almost to the sides, and your hands should face downward from your shoulders, forming a smooth curve. Be careful not to slump your shoulders.

Third Position. Place the heel of one foot in front of the middle of your other foot. Hold one arm curved in front of your body. The other arm should curve out to one side as it does in second position. This position is used in beginning ballet classes as a way to train your feet and legs for the fifth position, which is much more difficult.

Fourth Position. Cross one foot in front of the other with a space between them that is the length of your foot. Your feet should be turned out as they are in the first, second, and third positions. Extend one arm in a gentle curve in front of you. Raise the other arm so that your fingers form a graceful curve above your head.

Fifth Position. In fifth position, put the heel of your front foot against the toe or the joint of your big toe of your back foot. Keep both feet turned out. This is the most difficult of the five positions. Bring both arms up to form a graceful curve over your head. Your fingers should be relaxed but extended. Keep your shoulders relaxed.

DON'T FORGET ABOUT YOUR HANDS!

When you dance your hands should never be stiff. Instead, they should be relaxed and graceful. In most ballet positions you will either keep your fingers softly cupped together or extend them to complete the smooth line you create with your arms. Hand gestures are very important in **mime,** which you will learn about later in this book.

A **barre** is a long wooden rail attached to the walls of a dance studio. Working at the barre gives you support and helps you balance as you stretch and practice basic positions to warm up your muscles. This prepares you for more complicated practice in the center of the room.

Barre work is usually made up of a series of movements that are repeated many times each day. This may sound boring, but most dancers enjoy it as part of their daily practice routine. The combination of movements becomes more complex and requires greater strength and flexibility as the dancer becomes more advanced. Most studios have mirrored walls so that students can watch themselves as they do their barre work. They can see in the mirror what they are doing well and where they may need to improve.

Hold the barre lightly and keep your elbows loose and low so that your shoulders stay relaxed. Your arm should create a gentle curve, not a sharp angle.

Be sure to properly warm up and stretch your muscles before starting barre work, such as the move this girl is performing.

BARRE WARM-UP: THE PLIÉ

Barre exercises help warm and loosen up a dancer's muscles. Tight muscles can lead to injuries, so dancers must take the time to warm up properly. One of the most basic barre exercises is the **plié**. The word plié comes from the French word *plier,* meaning "to bend." Practicing pliés builds your strength and flexibility and helps you develop proper **alignment.**

1 Face the barre and hold it lightly with both hands. Use it only to steady yourself.

2 Your feet should be turned out in first position.

3 Imagine that a vertical line connects your heels, hips, and head so that you are not leaning forward, backward, or to either side. Imagine the line traveling upward so that your torso rises away from the floor and does not sink as you plié.

4 Keeping your heels on the floor, slowly bend your knees so that they go directly over your toes. This position is called a **demi-plié.**

5 As you return to first position and straighten your legs, imagine that you are being pulled upward by a string to rise until the backs of your knees are completely straight. Always straighten your knees by lifting them rather than pushing them back.

6 With your feet still in the first position, roll up onto your toes and rise up to balance in the **demi-pointe** position on the balls of your feet. Imagine that your heels are being pulled together as if they are attached by a rubber band. Lower your heels slowly to the floor and repeat the movements.

Center practice usually comes after practice at the barre. Its main purpose is to train dancers for performing onstage. It is done in the center of the room, so dancers have a larger area in which to move. Without holding the barre they can change directions and dance through the space.

This is the typical order many dancers use for their center work:

1 *port de bras* (arm exercises)

2 *adagio* (slow movements that require balance and control)

3 *pirouettes* (turns and spins)

4 *petit allegro* (small, brisk movements, including jumps)

5 *batterie* (quick jumps in which the feet or calves are beaten together during the jumps)

6 *grand allegro* (large, brisk movements, including jumps)

7 *pointe work*

This dancer is performing a grand jeté, which is an example of grand allegro.

A dancer's feet will change from one position to another in midair when he or she performs the batterie.

DIRECTIONS OF THE BODY

Beginning with their early training, ballet dancers learn the French terms for the directions of the body. These tell the dancer the direction of movements and positions in relation to an audience sitting in front of the dancer.

Croisé means that the dancer's legs are crossed at an angle in relation to the audience.

Devant means a position in front of the body.

Derrière means a position behind the body.

Écarté means "thrown wide apart." The body is positioned diagonal to the audience.

Effacé means "shaded." The dancer stands at an angle so that part of the body is hidden or shaded from the audience.

Épaulement is a position in which the dancer places the shoulders and head relative to the hips to add beauty or expressiveness to a step or movement.

Croisé Derrière

Écarté Derrière

Effacé Derrière

Dancers and other performers also follow stage directions. These directions tell them which area of the stage they are moving to and from.

- **Upstage**—the part of the stage farthest away from the audience (US)

- **Downstage**—the part of the stage closest to the audience (DS)

- **Stage left**—Facing the audience, the area of the stage to the dancer's left (SL)

- **Stage right**—Facing the audience, the area of the stage to the dancer's right (SR)

Your teacher may use these terms in class or when you are getting ready to perform for an audience.

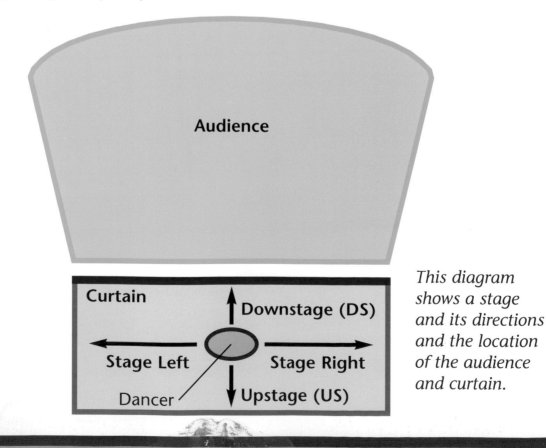

Audience

Curtain

Downstage (DS)

Stage Left — Stage Right

Dancer

Upstage (US)

This diagram shows a stage and its directions and the location of the audience and curtain.

DANCERS ON THEIR TOES

Even if you have never been to a live ballet performance, you have probably seen pictures or films of dancers gracefully spinning on the points of their toes. This is called dancing on **pointe.** It is one of the most magical sights in all of ballet. It is also very difficult to do and can cause serious injury for dancers who are not properly trained for it. Your teacher will use careful judgment to decide if and when you are ready to dance on pointe. Only female dancers perform pointe dancing.

Dancing on pointe requires dancers to wear shoes with specially built-up toes. Dancers usually begin their pointe training by doing exercises at the barre. As their legs and feet get stronger, they move their practice out to the center of the room. In most cases it takes many years of study and practice before a dancer is ready for pointe work.

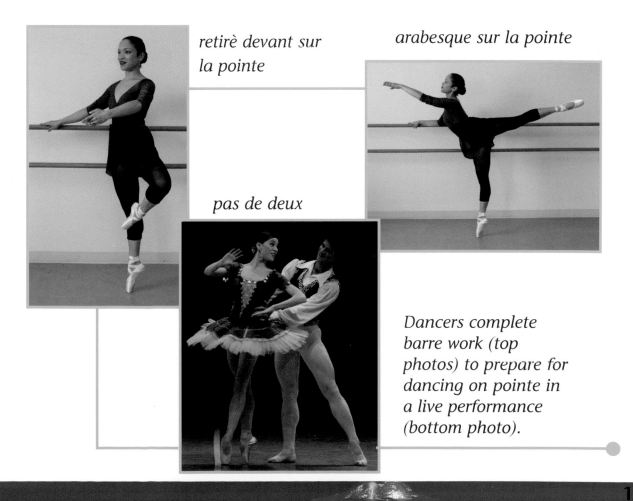

retirè devant sur la pointe

arabesque sur la pointe

pas de deux

Dancers complete barre work (top photos) to prepare for dancing on pointe in a live performance (bottom photo).

- If you only take one ballet class per week you will probably do some of your dancing at home. There are a few things you will need to do to dance safely and effectively at home.

- First, talk with your teacher and ask for advice about what you should work on. During home dancing do only the movements your teacher assigns to you. When you return to class, you can ask your teacher whether you have improved.

- With the help of your teacher and another adult, create a practice schedule.

- With an adult's help, create your home dance space. If the floors at your house are slippery, you will need a mat or a rug with a pad under it. Test it a few times before you begin dancing. Make sure the pad doesn't slip.

- Choose music that you enjoy.

- The rooms in your house are not likely to have railings attached to the walls, so you will have to create a substitute practice barre. The edge of a stable chair or four-legged table will do. Just make sure that you can rest your hands on it comfortably at about waist height. (This is only to help you balance—remember not to lean on it.)

A chair can provide good support for practice.

- Wear soft ballet slippers and your **leotard** and tights or other clothing that allows you to move around freely.

- Try to dance during a time when you are not likely to be distracted by siblings, pets, or household chores.

- Remember to drink plenty of water during your dance practice.

- Stick to your dancing schedule. Some people dance for only 15 minutes a day. Others dance for an hour or more. Do not dance to the point where you feel too tired to continue.

! ***If you feel any pain, stop what you are doing immediately.*** At your next class, ask your teacher for help with the problem.

Remember to take water breaks during practice.

If you feel pain when you practice, stop dancing at once. See a doctor or ask your teacher what to do.

FEELING THE MUSIC

Ballet is usually practiced and performed to music. The music **intensifies** the ideas and emotions of the dance. Some ballets use prerecorded music. Others depend on a live **accompanist,** band, or orchestra. If the music is performed live, there is a special relationship between the musicians and the dancers. They are all members of a team.

Dancers pay close attention to the music's rhythm and pace. Music will tell you whether to move quickly, slowly, or somewhere in between. Dancers do more than just *hear* the music. They *feel* it, too. As a dancer you must be aware of the music's rhythm, **tempo**, and mood. Ballet is all about using movement to express the emotions of the music.

This performance of Melody on the Move *clearly shows how ballet dancers use movement to express the emotions of the music.*

DANCING TO MUSIC

When you dance at home, choose different kinds of music as you move. For example, you might try dancing one day to rock music, the next day to hip-hop or country and western, and the day after that to African drumming or a classical violin concerto.

Before you begin dancing, listen to the music for a few moments. Let the sound set the tempo and the feeling of your movements. If you are listening to a series of slow musical notes, you might try a different foot and arm position every time the notes change. Or you might do a very slow **plié** in time to the music.

When you dance to faster music, let the tempo change the pace of your movement. You may want to do a series of quick pliés. Always make sure you are properly warmed up first. Never move so quickly that you pull a muscle. Whether you are in class or dancing at home, if you feel pain of any kind, stop the movement immediately.

You can choose what type of music you want to dance to when you practice at home.

PLAYING A ROLE

In many ways, a dancer in a ballet is like an actor in a play. Both the dancer and the actor play a role. Unlike a play, however, ballet does not use words to tell a story. Instead, it uses movement and music.

Ballet depends on a blend of physical expressions. They include classical movements and positions, **mime,** and natural body language.

MIME

Traditional mime uses specific **gestures** to reveal **emotion** or action. These movements are usually carried out exactly the same way each time. Here are some examples:

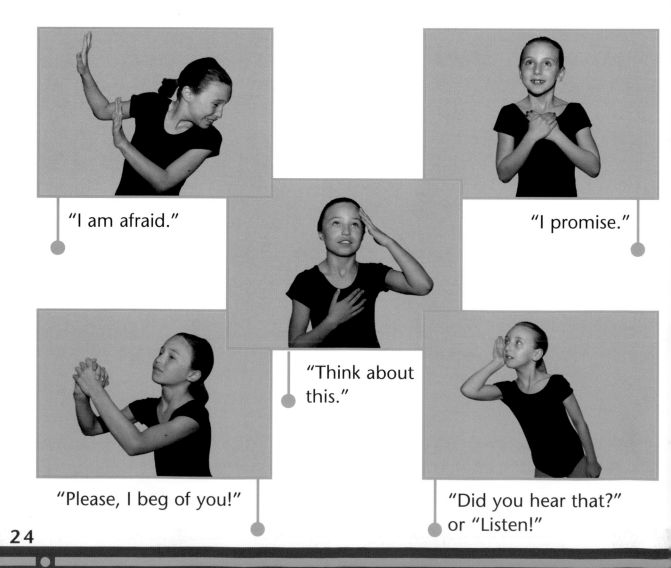

"I am afraid."

"I promise."

"Think about this."

"Please, I beg of you!"

"Did you hear that?" or "Listen!"

Dancing with a partner will introduce you to an entirely new side of ballet.

DANCING WITH A PARTNER

If you continue to study ballet, the chances are that you will one day be asked to dance with a partner. A dance with a partner is called a pas de deux. When you dance with a partner, you have to keep in mind not only your own movements, but also those of your partner and the overall picture the two of you are trying to create.

Dancing with a partner can be fun and exciting. In a way, you are responsible for one another's success. That is a big responsibility! You are individual dancers, but together you form a team. So it is important that the two of you develop a special bond of trust. This bond will come from each of you knowing your movements, practicing together over and over again, using eye contact, and talking things over whenever necessary.

This pair of dancers performed in a ballet in Miami, Florida.

RECITALS AND PERFORMANCES

After many weeks, months, and sometimes years of classes and practice, your teacher may invite you and your fellow ballet students to take part in a public performance called a **recital**. Performing is fun and exciting.

Here are some things to keep in mind when you perform.

- Performance is the time to have fun! It is not the time to worry about your dancing. **Rehearsal** is the time to worry about mistakes. Just know all your hard work will carry through!

- If you do make a mistake, do not worry about it. Everyone makes mistakes. Just keep dancing in rhythm and stay in your character. It is likely that no one will notice.

- If you totally forget what to do, follow someone else or make up your own movements until you remember your role.

- A little nervousness can be a good thing because it gives you added energy and excitement. If you are very nervous, remember that everyone in the audience is happy that you are dancing. They are there to support you.

- Sometimes the stage floor can be slippery. If that is the case, you will probably need to use rosin, a sticky white powder you can apply to the bottom of your ballet slippers to keep from slipping on the stage.

- Great dancers, like great athletes, can make even the trickiest moves look easy. Often a dancer's face is the first place to show the strain. Try to keep your face relaxed as you dance.

Professional ballet **companies** rarely invite their students to perform for the public. Instead, these schools hold open classes in which the public is invited into the studio setting to watch a class in progress.

WHEN YOU ARE BACKSTAGE ...

The stage is a special place. The areas behind and to the sides of the stage are called **backstage.** This is where dancers wait before making an **entrance.** It is also where they go when they leave the stage. Backstage **etiquette** is important. Here are some rules to keep in mind.

- Try to stay calm while you wait to go onstage. It is natural to be a little nervous when you perform, but remember to breathe and maintain proper **alignment.** If you feel yourself getting overly tense, take a couple of very deep breaths or do some simple stretches to loosen up.

Dancers often get mentally prepared for a performance backstage.

- Be polite and encouraging to your fellow dancers. Do not criticize others if they make mistakes. Remember that you are all working together. Treat your fellow dancers the way you would like to be treated yourself.

- Always stay alert and quiet backstage. Missing an entrance or coming onstage too early can be embarrassing and can get in the way of other dancers' performances.

Notice how relaxed this dancer looks. Try to stay relaxed when you are preparing to go onstage.

Today ballet is popular all over the world. Among the oldest ballet **companies** are the Paris Opéra Ballet (founded in 1661), the Royal Danish Ballet (Copenhagen, Denmark, founded in 1748), the Kirov (St. Petersburg, Russia, founded in 1783), and the Bolshoi (Moscow, Russia, founded in 1856). But there are also ballet companies in Asia, South America, Europe, and Africa. Every ballet company has its own special quality

All ballet companies have an associated school so that students can learn the company's **technique** and style. Graduates of a ballet school may dance for its company or find jobs in different companies. In this way, ideas and methods are exchanged throughout the dance community.

These dancers are shown in 1994 at the Paris Opéra Ballet, the world's oldest ballet company. Roland Petit, a famous dancer and **choreographer**, *is in the background.*

Each company, such as the Bolshoi Ballet, brings its own special style and spirit to the ballet.

In March 2003, the Kennedy Center in Washington, D.C., hosted a two-week International Ballet Festival. Audiences were treated to performances by some of the world's greatest ballet companies, including the Bolshoi, the Royal Danish Ballet, the Kirov, and the American Ballet Theater.

The Dance Theater of Harlem was founded as a place for talented African-American ballet dancers to train. The company and the school have become world famous.

As time goes on, ballet will continue to change and grow. Ballet companies exchange ideas, **traditions**, and even dancers. The result is a lively art form that captures the hearts and minds of dancers and audiences alike.

The Kirov Ballet is shown here performing a piece from the ballet La Bayadere.

Dancers often take bows in front of the audience after their performances, like these dancers in Russia.

GLOSSARY

accompanist	musician who plays during dance rehearsals or performances
alignment	how body parts are arranged in relation to other body parts
athletic	of or relating to athletes or athletics, which are games, sports, and exercises requiring strength and skill
ballet master	person who is responsible for teaching the choreography to be performed by a company
barre	waist-level bar that dancers use for support
choreographer	creator of dance compositions and ballets
company	organization of dancers or other performers
contemporary	modern or present-day
demi-plié	movement in which the knee is bent until the thighs and legs form a 45 degree angle
demi-pointe	foot position in which the dancer balances with toes flat on the floor and heels lifted up off the floor
entrance	point at which a dancer comes onto the stage
etiquette	rules governing the proper way to behave
flexible	able to bend easily
gesture	movement of body, arms, or legs that expresses an idea or feeling
hyperextended	extended beyond a normal angle
intensifies	strengthens
interpretation	artistic explanation or translation made through a performance or adaptation
leotard	snug bodysuit made of stretchy material
mime	using actions and body movements to tell a story without speaking words
placement	alignment of the body. When a dancer uses proper placement, he or she will be standing up straight with the hips level and even. The shoulders should be open but relaxed and centered over the hips. The pelvis and back should be straight, and the head should be up. The body's weight should be centered evenly between the feet.
plié	bending of the knee or knees
pointe	dance movements performed on the tips of the toes using reinforced shoes. Performing these dance movements is known as dancing on pointe.
pointe shoes	ballet shoes with specially built-up toes for dancing on pointe
professional	person who takes part in an activity for money rather than for fun
recital	public performance by dance or music students

rehearsal	private practice of dance to prepare for a public performance
royalty	members or relatives of a royal family
technique	manner in which body movements are made
tempo	musical pace or speed
tradition	handing down of beliefs, customs, or information from one generation to the next
turnout	ability of ballet dancers to turn their feet and legs out from the hip joints to a 90 degree position

MORE BOOKS TO READ

Augustyn, Frank, and Shelley Tanaka. *Footnotes: Dancing the World's Best-Loved Ballets.* Brookfield, Conn.: Millbrook Press, 2004.

Bowes, Debra. *The Ballet Book: The Young Performer's Guide to Classical Dance.* Westport, Conn.: Firefly Books, 2003.

Bussell, Darcey. *Ballet.* New York: Dorling Kindersley Publishing, 2000.

Friedman, Lise. *First Lessons in Ballet.* New York: Workman Publishing, 1999.

Varriale, Jim. *Kids Dance: The Students of Ballet Tech.* New York: Dutton Children's Books, 1997.

TAKING IT FURTHER

American Ballet Theater
890 Broadway
New York, NY 10003
(212) 477-3030

American Repertory Ballet
Princeton Ballet School
301 North Harrison Street
Princeton, NJ 08540
(609) 921-7758

Dance Theater of Harlem
466 West 152nd Street
New York, NY 10031
(212) 690-2800

Joffrey Ballet School
434 Sixth Avenue
New York NY 10011
(212) 254-8520

School of American Ballet
70 Lincoln Center Plaza
New York, NY 10023-4897
(212) 769-6600